HANDY CRAFTS

RAINY DAY FUN

Gillian Souter

Gareth Stevens Publishing
A WORLD ALMANAC EDUCATION GROUP COMPANY

★ Before You Start ★

Some of these projects can get messy, so make sure your work area is covered with newspaper. For projects that need paint, you can use acrylic paint, poster paint, or any other kind of paint that is labeled nontoxic. Ask an adult to help you find paints that are safe to use. You will also need an adult's help to make some of the projects, especially when you have to stitch fabric, poke holes with pointed objects, use a craft knife or any other sharp cutting utensils, or bake something in an oven.

Please visit our web site at: www.garethstevens.com
For a free color catalog describing Gareth Stevens Publishing's
list of high-quality books and multimedia programs,
call 1-800-542-2595 or fax your request to (414) 332-3567.

Library of Congress Cataloging-in-Publication Data

Souter, Gillian.
    Rainy day fun / by Gillian Souter.
       p. cm. — (Handy crafts)
    Includes bibliographical references and index.
    Summary: Provides directions for creating a variety of items, including kirigami flowers, picture frames,
greeting cards, decorated boxes, and stenciled T-shirts.
    ISBN 0-8368-3052-0 (lib. bdg.)
    1. Handicraft—Juvenile literature. [1. Handicraft.] I. Title. II. Series.
TT160.S653   2002
745.5—dc21
                                                  2001055087

This edition first published in 2002 by
Gareth Stevens Publishing
A World Almanac Education Group Company
330 West Olive Street, Suite 100
Milwaukee, Wisconsin 53212 USA

This U.S. edition © 2002 by Gareth Stevens, Inc. Original edition published as *Rainy Day Crafts* in 2000 by Off the
Shelf Publishing, 32 Thomas Street, Lewisham NSW 2049, Australia. Projects, text, and layout © 2000 by Off the
Shelf Publishing. Additional end matter © 2002 by Gareth Stevens, Inc.

Illustrations: Clare Watson
Photographs: Andre Martin
Cover design: Joel Bucaro and Scott M. Krall
Gareth Stevens editor: JoAnn Early Macken

Printed in the United States of America

1 2 3 4 5 6 7 8 9 06 05 04 03 02

Contents

Wet Weather Gear 4
Kirigami Papercuts 6
Super Scrapbook 8
Veggie Prints 10
Chains of Steel 12
Stuck on You! 14
Melody Makers 16
Craft-a-Card 18
Treasure Chest 20
By the Book 22
Tissue Issue 24
Pencil Pals 26
Magic Muffins 28
Indoor Garden 30
Dream Catcher 32
Coin Can 34
Stylish Stencils 36
Wind Twirlers 38
Pompom Pomp 40
Light Show 42
Splatter Saver 44
Framed! 46
Glossary 48
More Craft Books 48
Index 48

Wet Weather Gear

Keep a supply of crafty odds and ends on hand. When the weather gets wild, you'll be ready for anything!

Save cardboard tubes and boxes, glass jars, and plastic bottles. They could just be masterpieces in the making!

Markers, crayons, and paints come in handy for decorating your projects.

Use the right glue
for your projects.
White glue is good
for sticking many
things together.
A glue stick is not
as messy, but it is
not as strong, either.
To hold pieces of fabric
together, you might need
a special kind of fabric glue.

Felt is fun to work with
and is available in many
bright colors.

Buy packages of paper and
thin cardboard so you have
a good selection when you
start crafting.

After you finish a craft
project, put away all the
leftover materials for the
next rainy day!

Kirigami Papercuts

Clip and snip a snazzy snowflake, a fancy flower, or a delicate design!

You Will Need
- scissors
- colored paper
- tape or string

1 Cut a square of colored paper. (You can make sure the paper is square by folding it diagonally.)

2 Fold the square in half to form a rectangle. Then fold it in half again to make a small square.

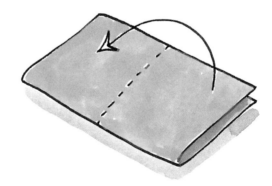

3 Fold the small square diagonally to make a triangle.

4 Snip small shapes from each edge of the triangle. Make sure you leave some of the folded edges uncut so the paper stays in one piece.

5 Unfold the paper to see the patterns you have created. Tape the square onto a window or tie some string to a corner of it for hanging.

★ **Bright Idea** ★
**Create a constellation
or a whole bouquet
of flowers!**

Super Scrapbook

Keep a decorative record of your special moments so you can remember them forever.

1 Cover a notebook with wrapping paper or with paper you have painted yourself.

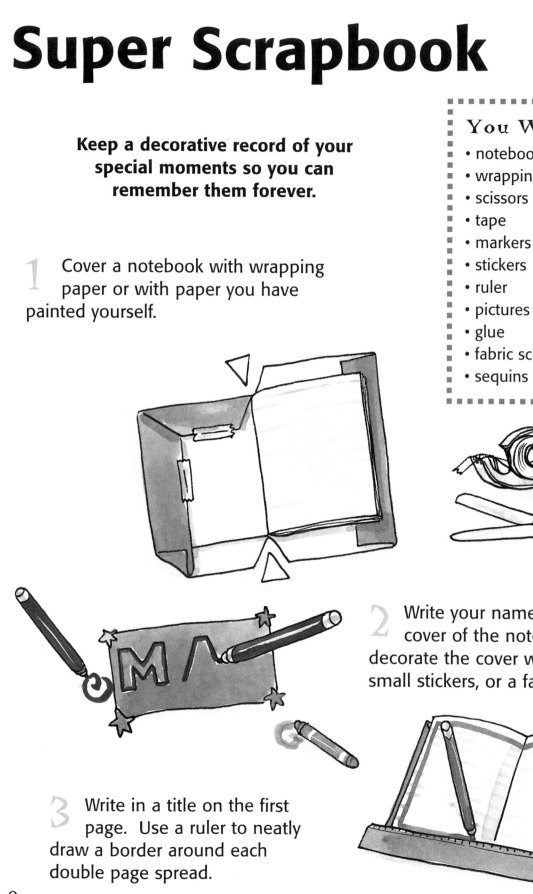

2 Write your name on the front cover of the notebook and decorate the cover with swirls, small stickers, or a fancy border.

3 Write in a title on the first page. Use a ruler to neatly draw a border around each double page spread.

4 Gather photographs or pictures from postcards or magazines. Cut out the pictures and glue them in place.

5 Add stickers and glue on fabric scraps, sequins, and other flat decorative materials. Fill the pages as much as possible.

★ Helpful Hint ★
Choose a theme, such as friends, school, or a special occasion, for each double page spread.

Veggie Prints

Print a delicious vegetable-stamp design to wrap up a special present!

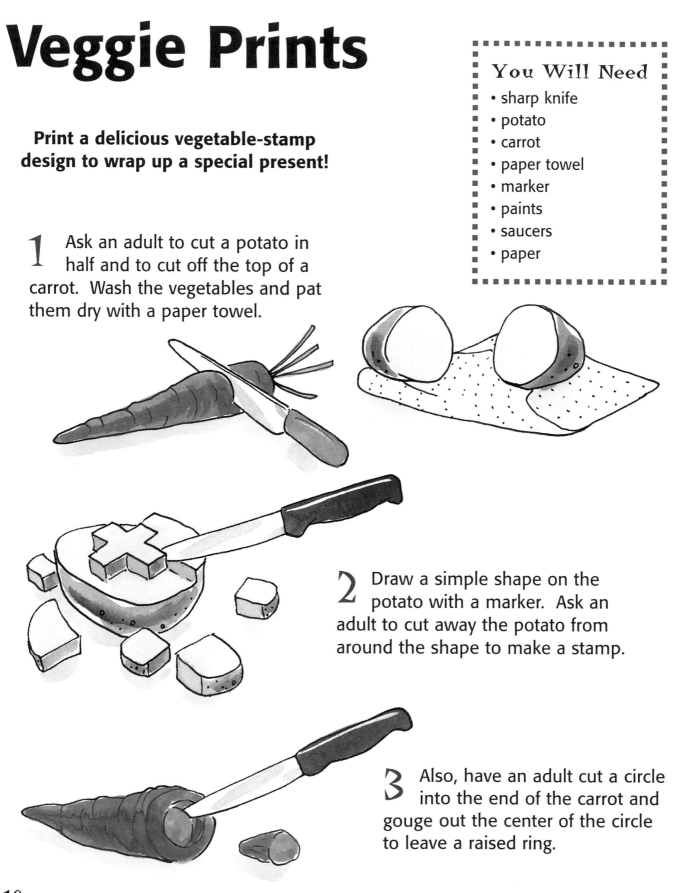

1 Ask an adult to cut a potato in half and to cut off the top of a carrot. Wash the vegetables and pat them dry with a paper towel.

2 Draw a simple shape on the potato with a marker. Ask an adult to cut away the potato from around the shape to make a stamp.

3 Also, have an adult cut a circle into the end of the carrot and gouge out the center of the circle to leave a raised ring.

10

4 Pour paint onto a saucer. Press the cut edge of the potato or the carrot into the paint.

5 Press the vegetable stamp firmly onto a large sheet of paper. To change colors, press the stamp onto scrap newspaper until no paint is left on it. Then prepare another saucer of paint and dip the vegetable stamp into the new color.

★ **Bright Idea** ★
To add extra color, brush a light wash of paint over the paper before you stamp prints on it.

Chains of Steel

You Will Need

- paper clips
- scissors
- thin elastic
- clear tape

Clip together a snappy necklace and string a matching bracelet in shining silver, vibrant colors, or a combination!

1 To make a chain of paper clips, point all of the clips in the same direction and slip the end of one clip over the middle loop of another.

2 For a necklace, make three chains, each with fifteen paper clips. Link the end clips of all three chains to another single paper clip. Add five more clips onto the other end of the single clip.

3 Link the last of the five new clips to the loose ends of all three chains to make a circle. Put on the necklace by slipping it over your head or by unfastening a clip along the five-clip chain.

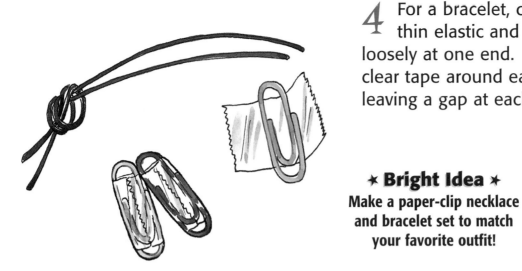

4 For a bracelet, cut two pieces of thin elastic and tie them together loosely at one end. Stick a piece of clear tape around each paper clip, leaving a gap at each end.

★ Bright Idea ★
Make a paper-clip necklace
and bracelet set to match
your favorite outfit!

5 Thread the pieces of elastic through the gaps in the top and bottom of each paper clip. Test the bracelet for size around the widest part of your hand, then untie the first knot and retie each piece of elastic, end to end.

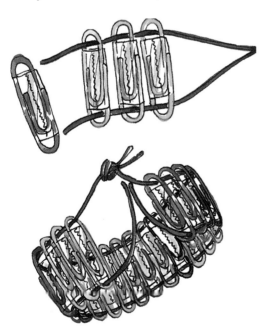

13

Stuck on You!

Turn your favorite photo into a marvelous magnet!

You Will Need

- magnet or magnetic tape
- scissors
- cardboard
- pencil
- photograph
- glue
- markers
- glitter
- stickers
- sequins

1 Peel the top layer off of an unwanted advertising magnet or cut a piece of magnetic tape.

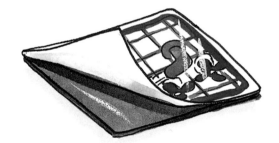

2 Lay the magnet on a piece of cardboard and draw around it. Cut out the shape.

3 Cut a small photograph and glue it onto the magnet.

4 Cut a window in the center of the cardboard. Glue the cardboard frame over the photograph.

5 Decorate the frame with markers, glitter, stickers, sequins, or any other eye-catching trimmings.

★ **Bright Idea** ★
Stick your magnets on the refrigerator to hold important messages.

15

Melody Makers

You Will Need
- plastic tub
- scissors
- large rubber bands
- soft drink can
- funnel
- rice or lentils
- tape
- paint
- paintbrush
- corrugated cardboard
- glue
- stiff cardboard
- ice cream stick

Sing along to a rainy-day song you can play on these improvised instruments.

1 A plastic tub or a strong box makes a simple stringed instrument. Cut five notches into the rim on opposite sides of the tub or box to hold the strings.

2 Stretch rubber bands over the tub so they fit into the notches. Play this musical string box by plucking the rubber bands or by strumming them with the front of your fingernails.

16

3   An empty soft drink can makes a great musical shaker. Wash out the can and let it drain. When the can is dry inside, use a funnel to pour in some rice or lentils.

4   Put tape over the opening of the can to keep the rice or lentils inside. Paint the outside of the can, and you're ready to shake a rhythm.

5   To make a scraper board, cut a long piece of corrugated cardboard, with the ridges running across it. Glue the corrugated cardboard onto a piece of stiff cardboard. To make music, run an ice cream stick up and down over the ridges of the corrugated cardboard.

★ **Bright Idea** ★
**Start a marching band
and have a parade!**

17

Craft-a-Card

You Will Need

- scissors
- colored cardboard
- craft knife
- ruler
- glue
- pencil
- sequins or foil candy wrappers

Send a glowing message in a gorgeous greeting card!

1 Cut out a rectangle of colored cardboard. Ask an adult to run a craft knife lightly down the middle, using a ruler to keep the cut straight. Fold the cardboard along the cut.

2 Cut out a cardboard square in a different color. Glue the square onto the front of the folded cardboard.

18

3 Draw a simple shape on another piece of cardboard. Cut out the shape and glue it onto the square.

4 Glue on sequins or cut pieces of foil candy wrappers to add some glitter to your greeting card.

★ Bright Idea ★
Fold a large sheet of paper, the same color as your card, to make a matching envelope.

Treasure Chest

Turn a boring box into a
classy case for your most
precious possessions!

1 Cover your work area with
plenty of newspaper. Paint
a box and its lid white and let
them dry.

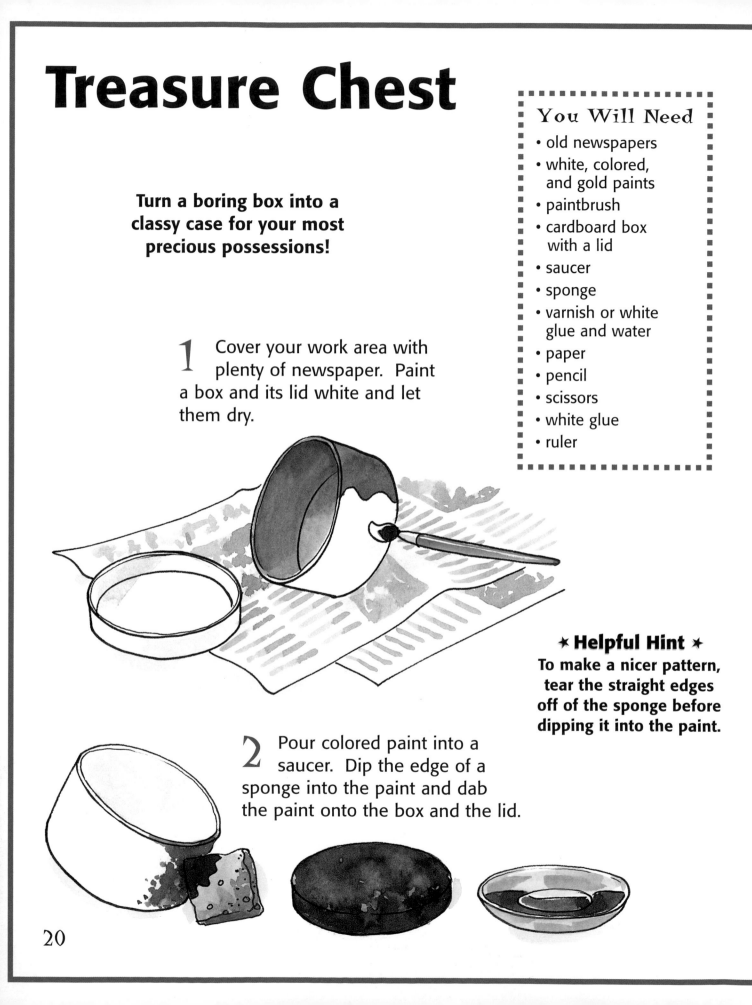

★ **Helpful Hint** ★
To make a nicer pattern,
tear the straight edges
off of the sponge before
dipping it into the paint.

2 Pour colored paint into a
saucer. Dip the edge of a
sponge into the paint and dab
the paint onto the box and the lid.

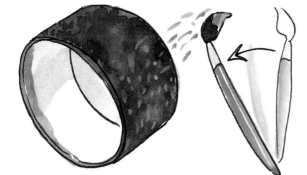

3 Dip a paintbrush into thin gold paint, then flick the paint at the box, turning the box and the lid so they will be covered evenly. When the paint is dry, brush on a coat of varnish, or white glue thinned with water, for a glossy finish.

4 Line the inside of the box with matching paper. First, draw around the bottom of the box. Then, cut inside the pencil lines. Glue this paper shape into the bottom of the box.

5 Next, measure the height inside the box and cut a strip of paper that wide. Glue the paper strip around the inside of the box.

By the Book

You'll never lose your place with this beautiful bookmark!

You Will Need

- ruler
- scissors
- felt
- pencil
- paper
- straight pins
- needle
- embroidery floss

1 Measure and cut a strip of felt that is 8 inches by 2 inches (20 centimeters by 5 cm). Fold the felt strip lengthwise. Snip off one end, diagonally, to make a point when you open the fold.

2 Draw a small shape on paper. Cut out this shape to use as a pattern.

3 Pin the paper pattern onto a new piece of felt and cut around it. Cut out several of these shapes this way.

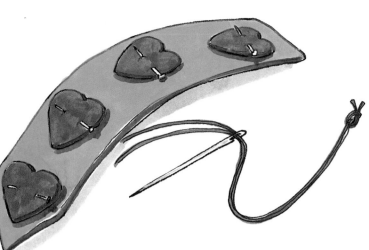

4 Pin the shapes onto the felt strip with the fold open. Thread a needle with two strands of embroidery floss and knot the end of the floss.

5 Sew the shapes onto the felt with neat running stitches. Tie a knot at the back to finish.

★ **Helpful Hint** ★
**Leftover scraps of felt
are perfect for
this project!**

Tissue Issue

This jewel of a jar makes an elegant vase, a handy pencil holder, or a useful utensil keeper.

1 Thin some white glue with a little water and coat the outside of a glass jar with the mixture.

2 Wrap the jar with aluminum foil. Trim around the rim with scissors.

3 Tear tissue paper into strips. Lay a strip over the jar and brush on some of the glue mixture to hold the strip in place. Continue gluing on strips until you like the way the jar looks.

4 Glue a wide strip of tissue paper around the neck of the jar, smoothing it down over the rim.

5 When the tissue paper is dry, seal it with another coat of the glue mixture.

★ **Helpful Hint** ★
If you use your decorated jar as a vase, try to keep the rim dry.

Pencil Pals

**Make a funny face
to keep you company
while you write!**

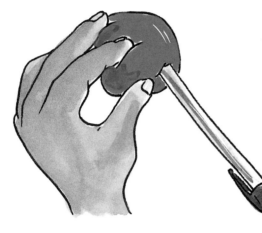

1 Soften some clay by kneading it with your hands. Roll the clay into a ball and gently push the end of a pen or a pencil into it.

2 Shape or cut other pieces of clay into features for a face, such as eyes, ears, nose, mouth, and so on.

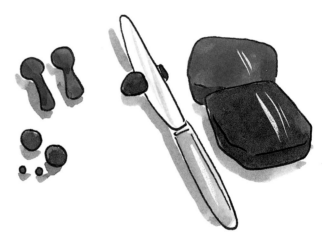

3 Press the features onto the head while the ball of clay is still on the end of the pen. When you finish making the face, carefully wiggle the head off of the pen.

4 Place the clay head in a baking pan. Ask an adult to help you bake it in the oven. Follow the baking instructions on the package of clay.

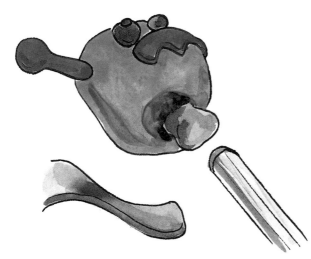

5 Let the head cool and turn hard. If it is loose when you put it back on your pen or pencil, put a small wad of modeling clay inside the hole before you push the pen into it.

★ **Bright Idea** ★
Make a special pencil pal for your favorite teacher.

Magic Muffins

**Warm up on a chilly day
with this sweet, baked treat!**

You Will Need

- 12 paper baking cups
- muffin pan
- kitchen utensils
- 2 cups (280 grams) self-rising flour
- 1/4 cup (60 g) butter
- 1 egg
- 3/4 cup (150 g) granulated sugar
- 3/4 cup (180 milliliters) milk
- 1 cup (200 g) chocolate chips
- powdered sugar

1 Ask an adult to preheat the oven to 400° Fahrenheit (200° Celsius). Put 12 paper baking cups in a muffin pan.

2 Sift the flour into a large bowl.

3 With a blunt knife, chop the butter into small pieces. Rub the flour into the butter. Make sure your hands are clean!

4 Lightly beat the egg with a fork, then stir the egg into the flour. Stir in the granulated sugar, the milk, and the chocolate chips.

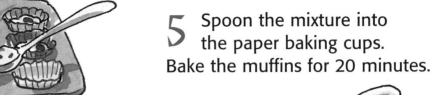

5 Spoon the mixture into the paper baking cups. Bake the muffins for 20 minutes.

6 Ask an adult to take the muffins out of the oven. Sprinkle them with powdered sugar and let them cool before serving.

★ Bright Idea ★
Substitute 1 cup (200 g)
of raisins, peanut butter chips,
or butterscotch chips for
the chocolate chips.

29

Indoor Garden

Bunches of these brilliant blooms can brighten up the darkest rooms!

1 Trace each part of this flower (left) separately on a piece of tracing paper. Cut out the pieces. Pin the tracings onto felt and cut around them. Cut two large flower shapes, one medium shape, one small circle, and four leaf shapes.

2 Push the end of a pipe cleaner through a cotton ball and bend the end back. Lay the cotton ball on a large flower shape.

3 Glue around the edge of the felt and lay the the other large flower shape on top of it. Press the edges of the flower together.

4 Glue on the medium shape and glue the small circle on top.

5 Cut a short piece of pipe cleaner and glue together a pair of leaf shapes around each end. Twist the pipe cleaner around the main stem of the flower.

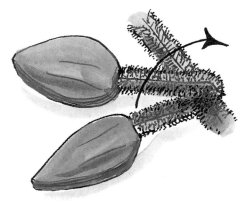

★ **Bright Idea** ★
Make a base for your bouquet by punching holes in a block of painted Styrofoam or a cardboard box.

Dream Catcher

**North American Indians
made these weblike hoops
to capture their dreams.
What will you capture in yours?**

You Will Need
- wire cutters
- wire coat hanger
- strong tape
- yarn or embroidery
  floss
- beads

1   Ask an adult to cut a piece of
wire from a coat hanger. Bend
the wire into a hoop and wrap strong
tape around the overlapping ends.

2   Tape the end of some yarn or
embroidery floss onto the hoop.
Wind the yarn or floss tightly around
the wire, knotting it now and then so
it will not unravel. When the wire is
completely covered, tie a tight knot.

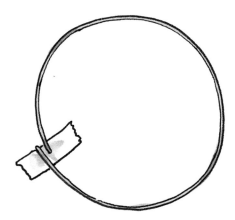

3   Knot more yarn or floss onto
the covered hoop. Pull it tightly
over to a point about a third of the
way around the hoop. Knot it at that
point, then repeat this step, pulling the
yarn or floss unevenly around the hoop.

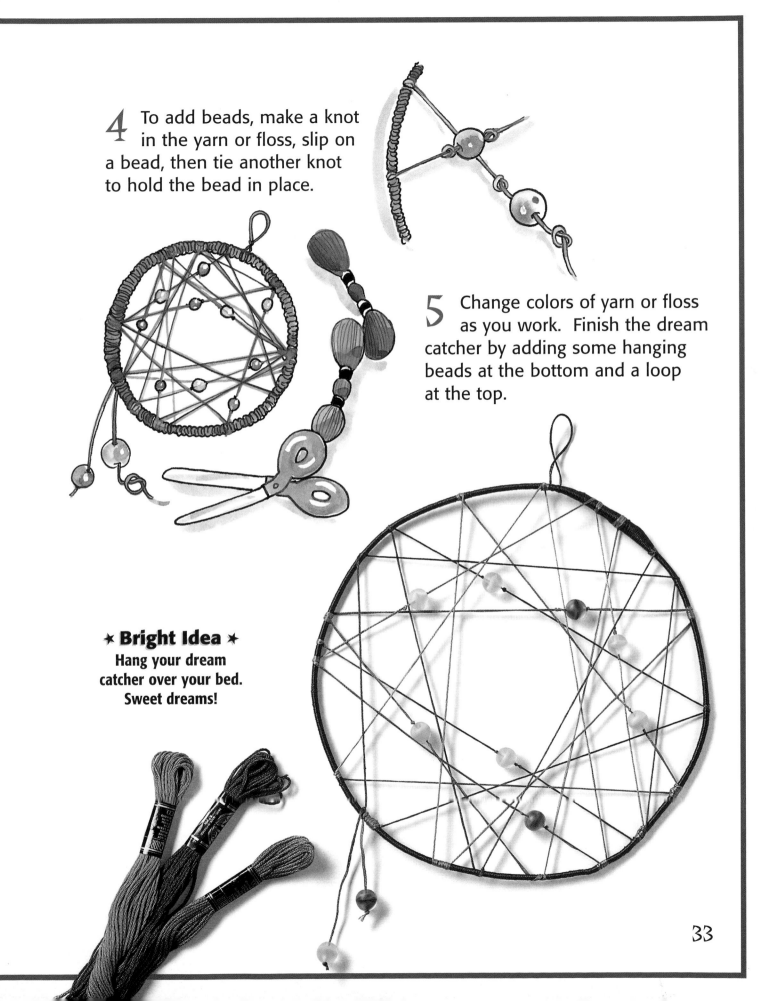

4 To add beads, make a knot in the yarn or floss, slip on a bead, then tie another knot to hold the bead in place.

5 Change colors of yarn or floss as you work. Finish the dream catcher by adding some hanging beads at the bottom and a loop at the top.

★ **Bright Idea** ★
Hang your dream catcher over your bed. Sweet dreams!

Coin Can

Collect your hard-earned cash in a coin-covered container!

1 Spread out an assortment of coins in a single layer on a table. Lay a sheet of white paper over the coins.

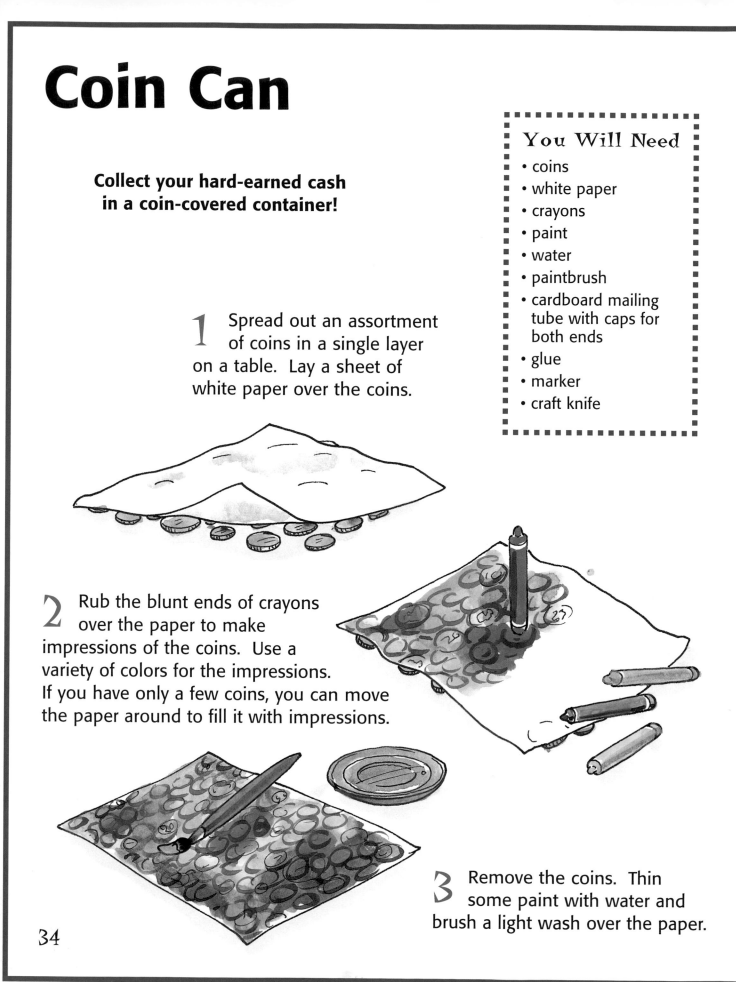

2 Rub the blunt ends of crayons over the paper to make impressions of the coins. Use a variety of colors for the impressions. If you have only a few coins, you can move the paper around to fill it with impressions.

3 Remove the coins. Thin some paint with water and brush a light wash over the paper.

34

4 Ask an adult to cut a cardboard mailing tube so it is slightly shorter than the coin-covered paper. Glue the decorated paper around the tube, tucking the ends neatly inside.

★ **Bright Idea** ★
To keep the outside of this colorful coin bank clean, add a coat of varnish.

5 Put a cap on one end of the tube. On the other cap, draw a thick black line that is slightly longer than your largest coin. Ask an adult to cut along this line with a craft knife to make a coin slot. Put this cap on the open end of the tube.

Stylish Stencils

Wear your art on your sleeves — and on the rest of your shirt, too!

1 Cut a piece of cardboard to fit inside a T-shirt. Put the cardboard into the T-shirt to keep the fabric flat and to stop paint from seeping through from one side to the other.

2 Draw a simple shape on a piece of stiff cardboard.

3 Ask an adult to cut out the shape with a craft knife to make a stencil.

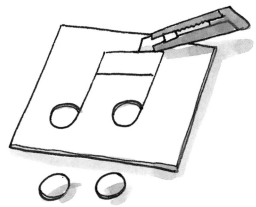

4 Pour some fabric paint into a saucer. Dip the corner of a sponge into the paint.

5 Lay the stencil on the T-shirt. Dab the sponge over the stencil until the shape is completely painted. Then, carefully lift the stencil, move it to another place on the T-shirt, and repeat the painting instructions. Let all the paint dry before you turn over the T-shirt to stencil the other side.

★ **Helpful Hint** ★
To paint thin lines, like the lines on the musical notes, apply the paint straight from its tube or bottle.

Wind Twirlers

You Will Need
- plastic bottle
- craft knife
- scissors
- paint
- paintbrush
- clear varnish
- hole punch
- string
- coat hanger or wooden skewers

They flip, they float, they fly! These curvy whirlers are as much fun to watch as they are to make.

1 Ask an adult to cut both ends off of a clean plastic bottle by making a slit in the side of the bottle with a craft knife, then using scissors to cut all the way around. Cut the middle section into several interesting shapes.

2 Paint small designs onto each shape. When the designs are dry, paint over them with a different color and let this base coat dry.

3 Paint on more designs over the base coat. (If you hold the plastic shape up to a window, you can see the first designs you painted.) When the paint is dry, brush on a coat of clear varnish.

4 Punch a hole in the top and the bottom of each shape. (The end shapes need only a top hole.) Tie pieces of string through the holes to join the shapes.

5 Tie several strings of plastic shapes onto a coat hanger or a cross made out of wooden skewers.

★ Bright Idea ★
Hang a wind twirler near a window and watch the shapes twist and turn in the breeze!

39

Pompom Pomp

Puffy pompoms will add the perfect punctuation to your fashion statement!

1 Trace over the two circles (above, left) in pencil. Lay the tracing facedown on stiff cardboard. Draw over the pencil lines. Cut out the cardboard ring. Make a second ring the same way.

2 Cut a long piece of yarn and tie one end around both rings. Wind the yarn around and around the rings (as shown). Cover the rings completely with yarn.

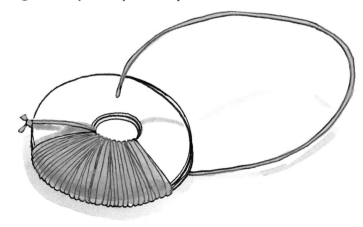

3 When the hole in the center gets small, thread the yarn onto a darning needle and keep winding.

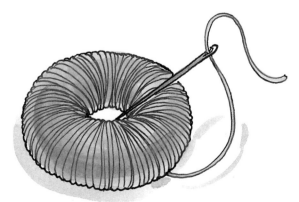

40

4 When the hole in the ring is full of yarn, snip the yarn between the two cardboard rings, all the way around.

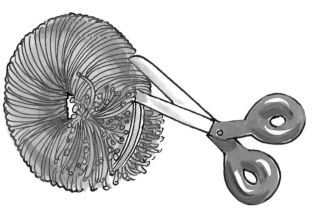

5 Tie a piece of yarn tightly around the middle of the yarn between the cardboard rings. Tear off the rings and fluff out the pompom.

6 To sew the pompom onto fabric, use a darning needle to pull the ends of the ties through to the back of the fabric. Then knot the ends and trim off the extra yarn.

★ **Bright Idea** ★
Decorate hats, scarves, shawls, blankets, socks – anything you want to wear!

Light Show

This lovely lantern glimmers and glows! Plan ahead to prepare for this project.

1 Remove the label from a clean tin can. Make sure the can has no sharp edges. Fill the can with water and leave it in the freezer overnight.

You Will Need

- tin can (such as a coffee can)
- water
- scissors
- paper
- pencil
- tape
- large rag
- nails
- hammer
- wire cutters
- wire
- candle

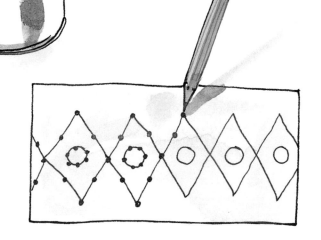

2 Cut a piece of paper the same size as the can's label and draw a simple pattern of dots on it. Take the can out of the freezer and tape the paper around it.

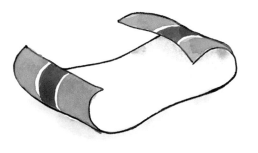

3 Lay the can on a rag in the kitchen sink to keep it from rolling around while you work.

42

4 Hold a nail over a dot and tap it
sharply with a hammer to punch
a hole in the can. Punch all of the dots,
working quickly before the ice melts.

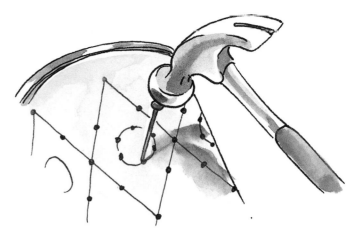

5 Punch two large holes opposite each
other at the top of the can near the
rim. Turn the can upside down in the sink
to let the ice and water drain out.

6 Cut and bend a piece of
wire for a handle. Bend
the ends of the wire sharply
and hook them through the
two holes on opposite sides
of the rim. Place a candle
inside your lantern.

★ **Helpful Hint** ★
To punch your pattern with
holes of different sizes, use
both large and small nails.

43

Splatter Saver

Don't worry about keeping your clothes clean. This pretty, practical apron protects them while you work!

You Will Need

- scissors
- newspaper
- ruler
- pen
- straight pins
- strong cotton fabric
- fabric paint
- needle and thread
- wide ribbon or cotton tape

1 Cut a piece of newspaper to 24 inches by 16 inches (60 cm by 40 cm). Fold it in half lengthwise. Draw a curve at one corner (as shown). Cut along the curve.

2 Open the newspaper and pin the paper pattern onto cotton fabric. Cut around the pattern.

3 Decorate the front of the fabric with fabric paint.

4 When the paint is dry, turn over the fabric. Fold over the edges, all the way around, and pin them in place. Sew along each edge with big running stitches.

5 Cut three 22-inch (55-cm) strips of wide ribbon or cotton tape. Sew one strip on each side (as shown). Sew the last strip at the top (as shown) to form a large loop.

★ Bright Idea ★
Decorate a cooking apron with food designs, a work apron with tool designs, or an art apron with drawing supplies.

Framed!

See yourself smile in this marvelous mirror with a textured frame!

You Will Need

- scissors
- thick cardboard
- ruler
- mirror
- pencil
- white glue
- tissue paper
- thick string
- water
- bowl
- newspaper
- paints
- paintbrush
- sponge
- clear varnish
- tape

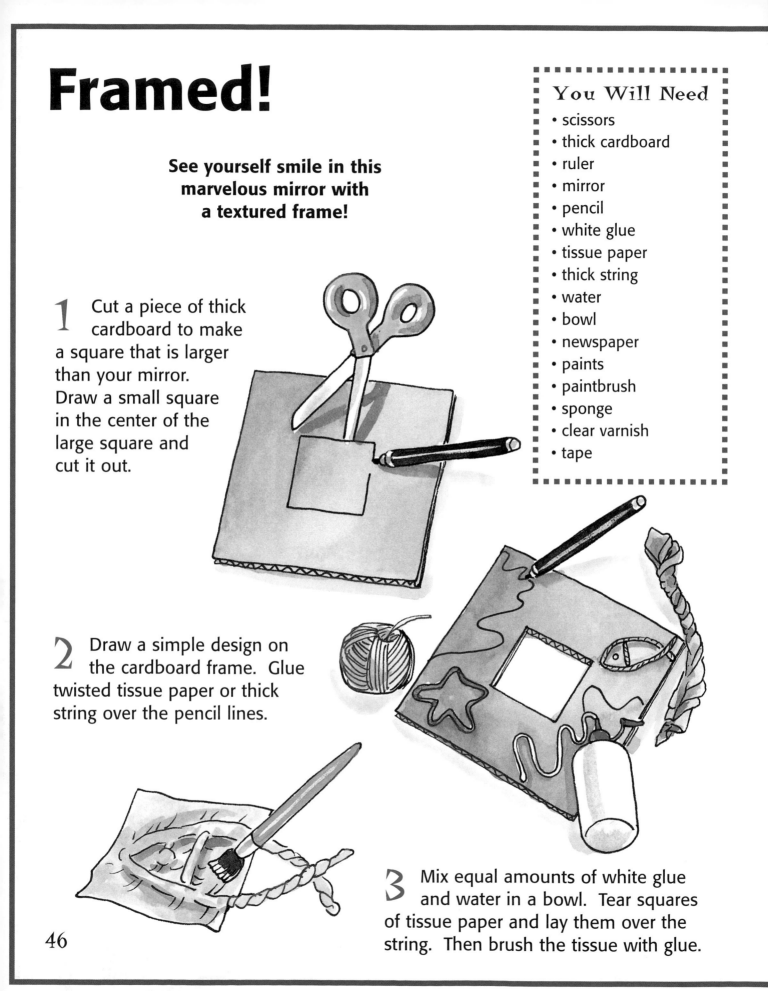

1 Cut a piece of thick cardboard to make a square that is larger than your mirror. Draw a small square in the center of the large square and cut it out.

2 Draw a simple design on the cardboard frame. Glue twisted tissue paper or thick string over the pencil lines.

3 Mix equal amounts of white glue and water in a bowl. Tear squares of tissue paper and lay them over the string. Then brush the tissue with glue.

46

4 Tear strips of newspaper. Paste overlapping strips, one at a time, over the rest of the cardboard and over all the edges. Let the frame dry.

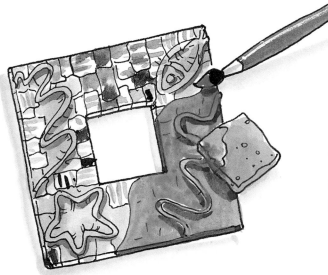

5 Paint the whole frame with a base color. When this paint is dry, paint with a sponge over the raised design, using a different color.

6 Brush on a coat of varnish. When the varnish is dry, tape the mirror onto the back of the frame, covering the hole.

★ **Helpful Hint** ★
Tape a loop of string to the back of the frame so you can hang the mirror.

Glossary

corrugated: having a wrinkled surface or a surface of ridges and grooves.

diagonally: in a slanting direction from one corner or side to the opposite corner or side.

embroidery floss: a soft, shiny thread made of several strands of silk or cotton, which is used to stitch designs on fabric.

impressions: the marks or outlines made by the pressure of harder or heavier objects against a softer surface.

improvised: made or put together on the spot, using whatever materials are readily available.

kirigami: the Japanese art of cutting folded paper to make delicate designs.

kneading: pressing and squeezing with the hands.

overlapping: lying over the top of something and partly covering it.

skewer: a pointed stick made of wood or metal, which is used to hold meat together while the meat is roasting.

stencil: a piece of stiff paper or cardboard with a design cut into it. When paint is spread over the stencil, the design is printed on the surface beneath it.

varnish: a sticky, paintlike substance spread over a surface to give it a hard finish and a shiny appearance.

wash: a brushed-on coating of watery paint.

More Craft Books by Gareth Stevens

Crafty Stamping. Crafty Kids (series).
  Petra Boase

Crafty T-Shirts. Crafty Kids (series).
  Petra Boase

Kids Create! Williamson Kids Can!® (series).
  Laurie Carlson

Paints Plus. Handy Crafts (series).
  Gillian Souter

Index

aluminum foil 24
aprons 44-45

baking 26, 27, 28
beads 32, 33
bookmarks 22-23
boxes 4, 16, 20, 21, 31
bracelets 12-13

candles 42, 43
cardboard tubes 4, 34, 35
clay 26, 27
coin banks 34-35
cotton 30, 44, 45
crayons 4, 34

dream catchers 32-33
drinking straws 16, 17

elastic 12, 13
embroidery floss 22, 23, 32, 33

fabric 5, 8, 9, 36, 41, 44, 45
felt 5, 22, 23, 30, 31
flowers 6, 7, 30-31
frames 15, 46-47

glitter 14, 15, 19
greeting cards 18-19

jars 4, 24, 25

kirigami 6-7

lanterns 42-43

magnets 14-15
mirrors 46, 47

mobiles 38-39
muffins 28-29
musical instruments 16-17

necklaces 12-13

painting 8, 17, 20, 21, 36, 37, 38, 44, 47
paper clips 12-13
pencil holders 24-25
pencil pals 26-27
photographs 9, 14, 15
pipe cleaners 30, 31
plastic bottles 4, 38
pompoms 40-41
printing 10-11

ribbon 44, 45

scrapbooks 8-9
sequins 8, 9, 14, 15, 18, 19
sewing 23, 45
skewers 38, 39
sponges 20, 36, 37, 46
stamping 10-11
stencils 36-37
stickers 8, 9, 14, 15

tissue paper 24, 25, 46
T-shirts 36-37

vases 24-25

wire 32, 42, 43
wrapping paper 8, 10

yarn 32, 33, 40, 41